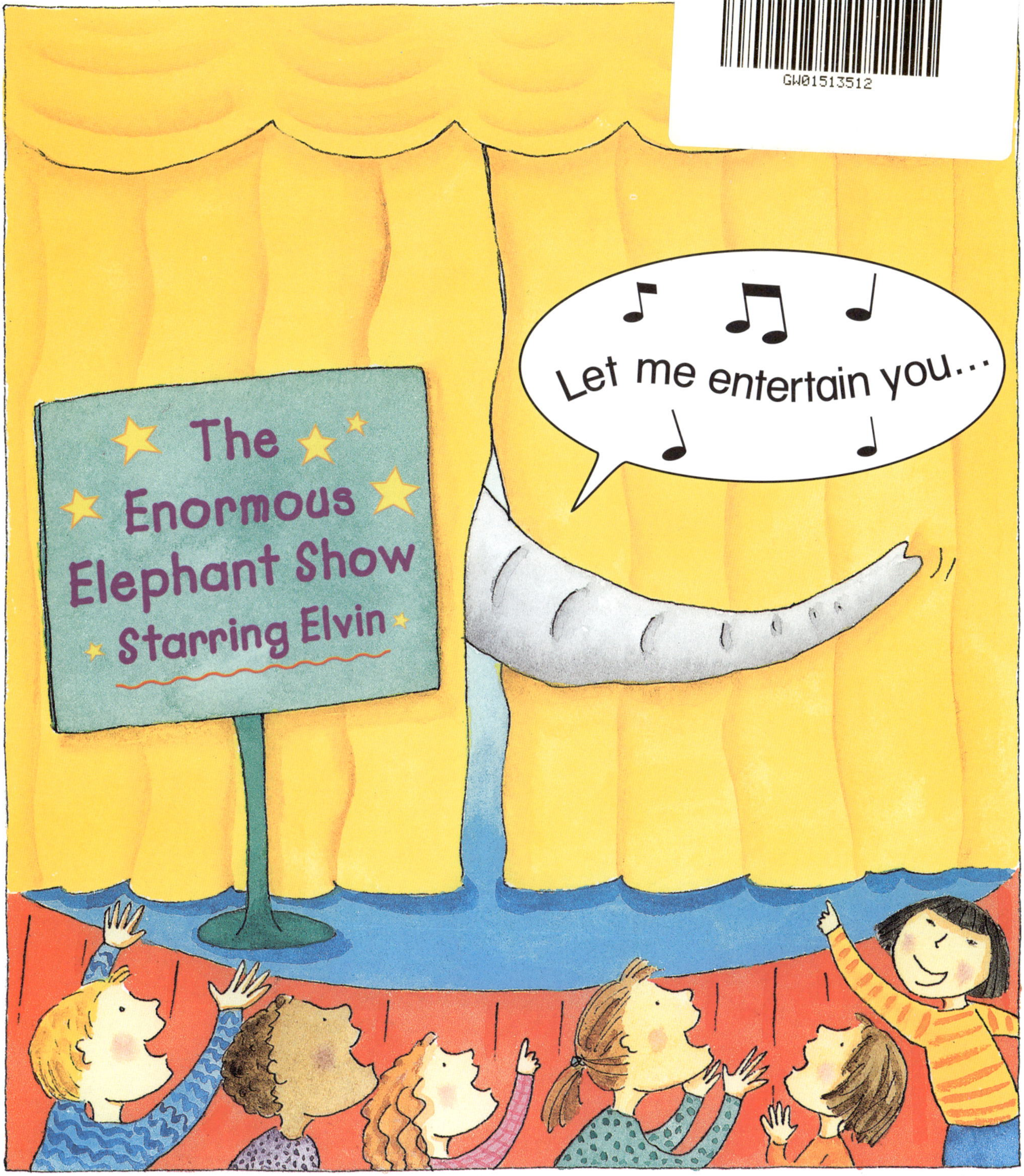

Elvin the Elephant is waiting backstage.
To start his show, just turn the page.

Elvin the Elephant makes an E out of eels!

Elvin the Elephant tosses eggplants to seals!

Elvin the Elephant does excellent dives!

Elvin the Elephant bakes elderberry pies!

Elvin the Elephant pulls an elk from a hat!

Elvin the Elephant sends e-mail to his cat!

Elvin the Elephant models elegant clothes!

Elvin the Elephant skates with eggs on his toes!

Elvin the Elephant climbs evergreen trees!

Elvin the Elephant eats a mountain of peas!

Elvin the Elephant exercises with a cow!

Elvin the Elephant takes an enormous bow!

How many things can you find that begin with the letter E?

See inside back cover for answers.

Ee Cheer

E is for elephant, E is for ear

E is for elk, a kind of deer

E is for egg, elbow, and eye

E is for eagle that soars through the sky

Hooray for E, big and small—

the most excellent, exciting letter of all!